Grade Boosters

BOOSTING YOUR WAY TO SUCCESS IN SCHOOL

QUESTIONS AND ANSWERS

First Grade

By Bailey Kennedy and Louise Howell

Illustrated by Jill Dubin

LOWELL HOUSE JUVENILE

LOS ANGELES

NTC/Contemporary Publishing Group

Published by Lowell House
A division of NTC/Contemporary Publishing Group, Inc.
4255 West Touhy Avenue, Lincolnwood (Chicago), Illinois 60646-1975 U.S.A.

Managing Director and Publisher: Jack Artenstein
Director of Publishing Services: Rena Copperman
Editorial Director: Brenda Pope-Ostrow
Director of Art Production: Bret Perry
Educational Editor: Linda Gorman
Project Editor: Joanna Siebert

Lowell House books can be purchased at special discounts when ordered in bulk for
premiums and special sales. Please contact Customer Service at:
NTC/Contemporary Publishing Group
4255 W. Touhy Avenue
Lincolnwood, IL 60646-1975
1-800-323-4900

Printed and bound in the United States of America

Library of Congress Catalog Card Number: 98-66550

ISBN: 1-56565-756-X

10 9 8 7 6 5 4 3 2 1

BOOSTING SUCCESS IN SCHOOL

The **GRADE BOOSTERS Questions and Answers** series is designed to build your child's confidence and motivation, while supplementing the instruction he or she receives in school. By allowing your child to experience learning in an enjoyable and stimulating way, this series helps your child develop the positive attitude toward learning that is necessary for academic success—and success in life.

Each introductory question and answer in **GRADE BOOSTERS First Grade Questions and Answers** is curriculum-based and grade-appropriate. Topics include social studies, science, art, math, and language arts. A series of follow-up questions develop children's critical and creative thinking skills, such as knowledge and recall, comprehension, deduction, inference, prediction, classification, problem solving, and creative expansion. These skills are essential for helping your child become a better thinker.

Two features appear throughout the book. TOGETHER TIME, designed for interactive learning, offers activities for you and your child to do together; the GRADE BOOSTER! feature provides activities and questions that further promote critical and creative thinking skills.

The inviting artwork on each page contains clues to some of the answers and provides visual reinforcement for learning. Suggested answers to the follow-up questions are included at the back of the book to help you guide your child.

Note to Parents

....

Time Spent Together

The time you spend with your child as he or she learns is invaluable. This "one-on-one" contact with your child cannot be duplicated at school. The more positive and constructive an environment you can create, the better. Here are some tips to keep in mind as you work with your child:

- Let your child look through the book and choose the questions or pictures that interest him or her. The questions in the book are self-contained and do not have to be done sequentially.

- Allow your child to go at his or her own pace. If your child wants to do only one or two pages, or answer only some of the follow-up questions, accept that and return to the material at another time.

- Give your child time to think about his or her answers. A common mistake parents and teachers make is to jump in with the answer when a child hesitates. Help your child by rephrasing the question if necessary, or by providing hints or prompts.

- Remember that your child's level of participation will vary at different times. Sometimes a response may be brief and simplistic; at other times, a response may be elaborate and creative. Allow room for both.

- Offer your child praise and encouragement frequently. It is much easier for a child to learn in a secure, accepting environment.

Positive experiences will strengthen your child's natural curiosity about the world and desire to learn. You have a prime opportunity to share with your child as he or she learns about the world around us.

What is a pattern?

A pattern is a set of designs, sounds, or actions repeated in the same order again and again. There are many types of patterns. For example, a colorful striped shirt has a pattern. The stripes appear over and over in the same order, such as red, gold, green; red, gold, green. Noises can also have a pattern, such as loud, soft; loud, soft. Patterns of actions are repeated movements, such as sitting, standing, jumping; sitting, standing, jumping.

1. The days of the week are repeated in the same order every week. How many days are in this pattern?
2. Look carefully around your home. What patterns can you find?
3. What kind of number pattern can you create? Say your pattern out loud.
4. On a separate piece of paper, design a pattern using different colors and shapes. How many shapes and colors did you use?
5. Invent your own action and word pattern that repeats two actions and two words, such as hopping on one foot two times, then saying the words **Hop! Hop!** How would you teach your pattern to a friend?

How many stars are in the sky?

There are billions of stars in the universe, but we cannot count all of these stars, or even see them all from Earth. *Astronomers,* the people who study the stars and planets, may be able to see more than one billion stars using very powerful *telescopes.* These special instruments make faraway objects, such as the stars and planets, appear to be closer and larger. Without using a telescope, we can see even fewer stars in the sky. That is because most stars are not bright enough, or they are too far away from the Earth, for us to see them. On a clear night, you might be able to see 3,000 stars in the sky.

1. Would it be better to count or *estimate*, which means make a guess, if you wanted to find out how many stars you can see on a certain night?
2. Can you see any stars during the day?
3. What is a star map?
4. Why do you think astronomers are excited about using a telescope that can be shot into space by a rocket?

5. Have you heard this rhyme before?

Star Light, Star Bright

Star light, star bright,
First star I see tonight,
I wish I may, I wish I might,
Have the wish I wish tonight.

Why do you think people sometimes make a wish when they see a star? What would you wish for if you saw a star?

TOGETHER TIME: Ask an adult to take you outside on a clear night to look at the stars. Try to find someplace where there are not very many lights. How do the stars look? Next, borrow a telescope, or ask an adult to take you to an *observatory,* a place where you can look at stars through a large telescope. How are the stars different from when you looked up at them without a telescope?

What is language?

Language is the set of signs, sounds, gestures, and marks that people use to understand each other. Language allows people to *communicate,* or share ideas, feelings, and information. More than 6,000 different languages are used in the world today. Each language has its own words and rules, so that people can use the language in the same way and understand each other. It would be very hard to communicate without language. Without language, there would not be any books, radio, television, or telephones.

1. Do you know another language besides English?
2. Do animals talk?
3. How would you communicate with someone who speaks a different language than you do?
4. What is sign language?
5. What language do most of the people who live in France speak? If you don't know, how can you find out?

Language Arts/Social Studies

How long ago did people start making music?

People have probably been making music for a long time. It is very likely that people have been singing for as long as they have been talking. Later, people may have used hunting tools as the first musical instruments. Music is the art of putting sounds together in an interesting pattern. People use music to express new ideas and feelings, such as joy, sadness, love, or anger. Today, many different types of music can be found around the world. In the United States, for example, a lot of people enjoy rock-and-roll, jazz, country, and classical music.

1. What is your favorite song? Why do you like it? How does this song make you feel?
2. What sounds do you hear when you are outside that remind you of music?
3. When and where do you usually hear music?
4. Why do you think people sometimes feel like dancing when they hear music?
5. Music is an important part of many other arts. What other types of art can you think of that use music?

Why do we use money?

We use money to buy things that we want or need. A long time ago, people didn't use money. They traded for things they could not make themselves. This only worked if each person wanted what the other person had to trade. To make it easier, people started to trade certain things that everyone wanted, such as shells, beads, feathers, and blankets. Later, people began using silver for trade because it was easy to carry and would not be damaged in the rain. After a while, people started making coins from different types of metal. This was the first form of money. Later, people began to use paper to make money as well.

1. Do you ever trade with a friend for something you want? What kinds of things do you trade?

2. When you go to a store to buy something, how do you know how much money to pay for the item?

3. What is a piggy bank? On a separate piece of paper, draw a picture of a piggy bank. Why do people save money?

4. Why do you think people used so many different items to pay for things long ago?

5. On a separate piece of paper, create your own paper money. What designs will you put on your money? How much will each paper bill you design be worth?

TOGETHER TIME: Set up your own store with an adult friend. Choose items to sell in your store, then decide how much each item should cost. Write down the price of each item on a separate piece of paper. Let your adult friend decide how much money you should have to play with. What can you buy with the money you have? Practice counting out the money for each item you decide to buy.

Math/Art

Who was the first American president?

George Washington was the first president of the United States. He was born in Virginia and had a long, successful military career. Washington was a strong, dependable leader in the Revolutionary War. After this war, the first American colonies became the United States of America. Washington helped build a strong government for the United States. The people chose George Washington to be the first president of the United States because they trusted him. He served as president for eight years.

1. Every year the American people celebrate George Washington's birthday on Presidents' Day. Can you find Presidents' Day on a calendar?

2. What is the capital of the United States? If you don't know, how can you find out? **Hint:** The capital is the city where the government that runs a country is located.

3. Who is the president of the United States right now?

4. George Washington is often called the "Father of the Country." What do you think that means?

5. If you were the president, what would you do to change the country?

Social Studies

What is a cloud made of?

A cloud is made up of tiny droplets of water, ice, and dust that stick together in the air. As more and more droplets stick together, the cloud grows larger. When they are heavy enough, the droplets fall to the ground as rain, hail, sleet, or snow. The type of water or ice that falls from a cloud depends on the temperature of the air. For example, if the air is cold, sleet or snow might fall. If the air is warm, rain or hail might fall.

1. Does it always rain when there are clouds in the sky? Why or why not?
2. What do thunder clouds look like? On a separate piece of paper, draw what you think they look like.

3. What is fog?
4. Where do you see dew? What is it?
5. What is weather? How do clouds help us to know what the weather will be like?

How do people tell time?

In the past, people looked at the Sun, Moon, and stars to tell what time it was. Today, people usually use clocks to tell the time. A clock measures time in equal lengths of hours, minutes, and seconds. A *dial clock* has a round face that contains the numbers *1* through *12*, with a little hand that points to the hour and a big hand that points to the minutes. A *digital clock* simply shows numbers for the time. We say A.M. when it is after midnight and before noon (3:00 A.M.). This is the morning. We say P.M. when it is after noon and before midnight (3:00 P.M.). This is the afternoon or evening.

1. Look at the clocks above. Which one is the dial clock? Which one is the digital clock? What time do these clocks show?
2. What time is it right now? Practice using A.M. and P.M. when you say the time.
3. Why do you think people wear wristwatches?
4. When do you need to know what time it is? On a separate piece of paper, make a list of all the reasons you might check a clock to see what time it is.
5. How is your heartbeat different from the ticking of a clock?

Math/Science

TOGETHER TIME: Sometimes it is hard to tell how much time it takes to do something without looking at a clock. Ask an adult to help you with this activity. Copy the list below onto a separate piece of paper. *Estimate,* or guess, the amount of time it will take you to do each of the things on the list. Then ask the adult to time you while you do each one.

	estimated time	actual time
Brushing your teeth		
Reading a paragraph in a book		
Drinking a glass of water		
Singing "Row, Row, Row Your Boat"		
Writing your name		
Saying the alphabet		
Counting to 100		

Why did people once use pictures to write?

People used pictures, or *symbols*, to write before they had words. In some languages, the symbols *represented*, or stood for, an object or an idea. For example, a picture of a woman represented a woman. At other times, symbols were used to represent the sounds the people made when they talked. Sometimes people carved entire picture stories and messages into stone walls or pottery.

1. Traffic signs often show symbols instead of words. Why do you think it is helpful to have symbols on traffic signs?

2. We use symbols in many different ways. For example, many math problems have symbols, such as +. Where else can you find symbols?

3. What do you think a symbol for a mountain might have looked like in one of the earliest languages? On a separate piece of paper, draw a symbol for a mountain.

4. The Egyptians built large pyramids that had *hieroglyphics* (Hi-ruh-GLIH-fiks), or pictures, carved on the walls. What do you think these buildings looked like? On a separate piece of paper, draw some pyramids with hieroglyphics.

5. How do you think people today are able to learn about these symbols from so long ago?

16

What is the equator?

The equator is an imaginary line that circles the middle of the Earth at its widest part. The equator is about 25,000 miles long. The equator divides the Earth into two equal parts. The half of the Earth that is north of the equator is called the Northern Hemisphere. The half of the Earth that is south of the equator is called the Southern Hemisphere. Even though it is imaginary, the equator is an important part of most maps and globes. The equator helps people understand where the continents and oceans are located.

1. What do you think the word **equator** means? **Hint:** Read the paragraph above one more time.
2. What continents does the equator run through? Look at a map or a globe to find out.
3. Is the United States north of the equator or south of the equator? If you don't know, how can you find out?
4. It is usually very hot in most places near the equator. Why do you think that is so?
5. What fraction would you use to show how much of the Earth is north of the equator?

What is a holiday?

A holiday is a special day set aside during which people rest or celebrate. People all over the world have holidays, but they don't always celebrate the same ones. In the United States, there are many different types of holidays. Some holidays *honor,* or show respect for, an important person, such as Martin Luther King, Jr. Other holidays honor a group of people, as on Mother's Day. Holidays may also remind us of something important that has happened. Independence Day is one example of this type of holiday. Sometimes people enjoy holidays by eating special foods, exchanging gifts, watching fireworks and parades, or spending time with family and friends. Many schools and businesses close for holidays.

1. What is your favorite holiday? What do you like to do during that holiday?
2. On what holidays do you usually see fireworks? Why do you think people like to see fireworks?
3. Why do Americans celebrate Thanksgiving?
4. If you could make up a new holiday, what would it be called? Who would you honor, or what would you remember, during this holiday? What would you do during the holiday?

5. Ask a friend to tell you about his or her favorite holiday. Do you celebrate the same holiday? Do you do the same things that your friend does on that holiday?

GRADE BOOSTER!

Do you know about any holidays that are celebrated in another country? Choose a country. Then find out what holidays are celebrated in that country by looking in an encyclopedia or another book at the library. When are the holidays? What do people in that country do during those holidays?

What is a compound word?

A compound word is a word that is made by putting two words together to create a new word. For example, if you put the word *rail* and the word *road* together, you make a new compound word—*railroad*. You can do this with lots of different words. Words such as *snowball, birdhouse,* and *watchdog* are all compound words.

1. Look at the picture combinations above. What compound words do the pictures form?
2. What are the two words you hear in the compound words **butterfly, sidewalk,** and **grandfather**?
3. Look in one of your favorite books. How many compound words can you find? Make a list on a separate piece of paper.
4. Can you make your own picture combinations for each of the compound words on the list you just made? Ask a friend to solve your riddles.
5. What other compound words can you make using one of the pictures above? Make a list of the new compound words on a separate piece of paper.

Language Arts/Art

Who made the first American flag?

According to legend, George Washington asked Betsy Ross to make the first American flag in 1776, long before he became president of the United States. Betsy Ross lived in Philadelphia and sewed flags during the Revolutionary War. Her uncle, George Ross, worked with George Washington to create the American flag. We don't know for sure whether or not Betsy Ross actually sewed this flag. Many people believe that the flag was really designed by a man named Francis Hopkinson.

1. Why do you think George Washington thought it was important to have an American flag?
2. What does the word **legend** mean?
3. Why do you think that people are not exactly sure who designed and sewed the first American flag?
4. What other kinds of flags have you seen? What did they stand for?
5. On a separate piece of paper, design a flag for a new country. What colors or shapes will you include on this flag? Will they form a pattern?

Social Studies/Art

What are the five senses?

The five senses are sight, smell, touch, taste, and hearing. In general, you see with your eyes, you smell with your nose, you touch with your hands, you taste with your mouth, and you hear with your ears. The five senses are responsible for how your body gets information about the world. This information is sent to your brain, which puts all of the information together and helps you figure out what is going on around you. The brain also uses information from other senses that keep track of changes inside the body. These senses tell your brain when you are hungry, thirsty, or tired. Like the five senses, these other senses help protect your body.

1. How would you describe an orange using each of the five senses?
2. Which sense is affected when someone is blind? How does a blind person read?
3. What senses do you use when you play the piano? Do you need all of these senses to play? Why or why not?
4. If you had to give up one sense, which one would you give up? Why?
5. Can you name one way each sense makes the world less dangerous for you?

Science

TOGETHER TIME: Ask an adult to put a blindfold over your eyes. Then let him or her lead you by the arm outside. How does it feel? What senses do you use to find your way when you cannot see? Are you more aware of sounds and smells now that you can't see? What do you hear? What do you smell? Touch things around you. Try to guess where you are before you take the blindfold off. How close were you to the place where you thought you were standing?

Why do people use maps?

Maps help people understand how the world is set up. People use maps to find certain places, measure distances, and plan trips. There are many different kinds of maps. A map might show a city, a country, or even the whole world with the oceans and the continents. A map has pictures, or *symbols*, that show where things such as bridges, airports, and campgrounds are located. A map also has a key, called a *legend*, that explains how to read the map symbols.

1. Have you ever read a map? What locations or information did it show?

2. Can you think of a time when you might need a map?

3. How are the compass directions of north, south, east, and west shown on a map?

4. What is the difference between a map and a globe? Should you use a map or a globe if you need to find out how to get to the park?

5. Close your eyes and imagine that you are a bird flying through the rooms in your home. On a separate piece of paper, can you draw a map of your home from this "bird's-eye view"?

Social Studies

Who was Pocahontas?

Pocahontas was a Native American girl born around 1595. Many people believe that Pocahontas bravely saved the life of John Smith when she was 12 years old, after Smith was captured by the warriors of Pocahontas's father, Chief Powhatan. John Smith was the leader of a group of people who moved from England to Virginia in 1607 to start a new home. These people were called *settlers*. Pocahontas wanted to create peace between the Native Americans and the settlers.

1. The name **Pocahontas** means "playful one." Does your name have a special meaning? What is it?

2. At times, the settlers and the Native Americans did not get along because they had such different ideas and beliefs. What are some beliefs the settlers had? What are some beliefs the Native Americans had? If you don't know, how can you find out?

3. What does the word **bravery** mean? Why do you think Pocahontas acted with so much bravery?

4. The settlers and the Native Americans sometimes traded. What kinds of things do you think they traded?

5. The settlers built homes that looked different from the homes the Native Americans built. How can you find out what these different homes looked like?

What is a contraction?

A contraction is a word that is made when two words are shortened and put together. One or two letters from the words are dropped and replaced with an apostrophe ('). You have probably seen or heard contractions, such as the word *isn't*, which is formed from *is* and *not*. With this contraction, the *o* in the word *not* is dropped and replaced with an apostrophe.

1. What are the two words the children on this page are using to make a contraction? What is the contraction that is formed?

2. Look in some of your favorite storybooks. What contractions can you find? Make a list of these contractions on a separate piece of paper.

3. Read your list of contractions. What two words were used to make each contraction?

4. Copy these words on a separate piece of paper:

   don't   **hasn't**   **she'll**

   Write the two words that were used to create each contraction. Circle the letters that were dropped to form the new contraction. What did you write in place of those letters?

5. Why do you think people sometimes use contractions?

❓ Are trees alive?

Trees are alive, but they are not like people or animals. Trees cannot move from place to place. A tree's roots lie underneath the ground. The roots take water from the ground and send it up through the tree to the leaves. A tree's leaves use water and light from the Sun to make the food that keeps the tree alive and helps it to grow. The trunk and branches on most trees grow thicker as the trees grow taller. Trees keep growing for as long as they live. Most trees live longer than any other plants. Some trees actually live for thousands of years.

1. What is a tree house? On a separate piece of paper, draw a picture of a tree house.
2. Do you think a tree feels pain when it is cut down? Why or why not?
3. In what ways are trees different from other plants?
4. What words can you think of that rhyme with the word **tree**?
5. Why do people think it is important to plant new trees?

Who was Mother Goose?

Nobody knows if there was ever a real Mother Goose. The collection of Mother Goose rhymes that we know today were probably written by many different people through the years. Mother Goose rhymes are poems, songs, and stories that have been told to children for a long time. Some people believe that Mother Goose was a real person and that she created these rhymes. Other people believe that Mother Goose is just a made-up character. Mother Goose is often shown as a woman or a goose with a big floppy hat. Here is a Mother Goose rhyme that you might already know.

Simple Simon

Simple Simon met a pieman
Going to the fair;
Says Simple Simon to the pieman,
Let me taste your ware.

Says the pieman to Simple Simon,
Show me first your penny;
Says Simple Simon to the pieman,
Indeed I have not any.

1. What other Mother Goose rhymes do you know?

2. These stories are fun to say out loud because the words at the end of the lines often sound the same, or rhyme. Look at the "Simple Simon" rhyme. Say the last word of each line out loud. Which words rhyme with each other?

3. What could you use to make a puppet to act out this "Simple Simon" rhyme? What actions would you make your puppet do as you recite the rhyme?

4. Read "Simple Simon" again carefully. What does the word **ware** mean in this rhyme?

5. Why do you think people would like to believe there was a real woman called Mother Goose?

GRADE BOOSTER!

What words can you think of that rhyme with **cat**? *Write your rhyming words on a separate piece of paper. How can you use them to create your own poem with rhyming words? Write down your poem. Now read your poem out loud. Clap your hands together or snap your fingers each time you say your rhyming words.*

What is a musical instrument?

A musical instrument is an object that is used to
create music. There are many different kinds of musical
instruments. Stringed instruments, such as the violin,
have strings that make different sounds when you touch
them with your fingers or a bow. Wind instruments are
tube-shaped instruments that you blow into while covering
certain holes to make different sounds. A flute is a wind
instrument. Percussion instruments, such as drums, make
sounds when you hit them with your hands or with a stick.
Keyboard instruments have keys that you press to make
different sounds. The piano is a keyboard instrument.

1. Have you ever played an
   instrument? What
   instrument did you play?
2. If you blew across the
   tops of three empty bottles
   that were different sizes,
   do you think you would
   hear the same sound from
   each one? Try it and see.
3. Have you ever seen a band play? What instruments were
   the people playing?
4. How is the way you play a wind instrument different from the way
   you play a stringed instrument?
5. Why do you think people enjoy playing different instruments
   together?

What are pioneers?

Pioneers are the first people to move into an area of land to set up a home. In America in the early 1800s, many people traveled to the west, where the land was not settled. These pioneers walked or rode on horseback. Later, pioneer families began to travel west in covered wagons that were pulled by horses. It was very dangerous for pioneers to travel through the wilderness. In a pioneer family, everyone had to help out. Sometimes pioneer children would carry water from rivers, milk cows, and help cook the food.

1. The pioneers could not bring many things with them when they moved. What would you bring if you were a pioneer to remind you of home?
2. Why do you think people would want to set up a home where the land was not settled?
3. Many pioneers traveled together in wagon trains. Why do you think they wanted to travel as a group?
4. Do you think it was hard to be a pioneer? Would you want to be a pioneer?
5. Why do you think people want to travel to space?

What do biologists do?

Biologists are scientists who study living things. They try to learn as much as possible about people, plants, and animals. Most biologists choose one particular thing to study. Some biologists study certain parts of the human body. Other biologists study diseases to help doctors figure out why people get sick. They try to find ways to make sick people better. Certain biologists even study the effects of space travel on human beings. A biologist might study plants in the rain forest to see which ones could be used to make medicine. Another biologist might try to find ways to help farmers grow better crops. Some biologists work with animals. They try to figure out how people can better protect the animals, and the environment, from harm. Biologists try to understand the relationships between people, plants, and animals, and the environment they live in.

1. If you were a biologist, what would you most want to study?
2. Where could someone who has studied biology work?
3. Look at the picture on the next page. What tool is the girl using? What kinds of things might a biologist look at with this tool?
4. Why would a national park be a good place for a biologist to learn about plants and animals?

5. Biology is an important field of science. What other kinds of things do people study in science? Do you know the names of any other fields of science? If you don't know, how can you find out?

GRADE BOOSTER!

Think about the last time you went to a playground. What kinds of living things did you see there that would interest a biologist? On a separate piece of paper, draw at least five things that live in a playground area that a biologist might want to study. How would a biologist study each of those things?

What is a fable?

A fable is a make-believe story that teaches a lesson. The characters are often talking animals who behave like people. One of the most well-known fables is about the tortoise and the hare. The hare bragged that he could beat the tortoise in a race. The hare ran very fast, but he stopped halfway through the race to eat and take a nap. The slow, steady tortoise kept walking without stopping. The tortoise crossed the finish line first and beat the hare!

1. How would you describe the tortoise? How would you describe the hare?
2. Why did the hare lose the race?
3. What do you learn from this fable?
4. What other fables have you heard?
5. Make up your own fable with talking animals. What lesson will your fable teach? What kinds of characters will you use?

What are continents?

Continents are the largest land masses on Earth. There are seven continents. From biggest to smallest, the continents are Asia, Africa, North America, South America, Antarctica, Europe, and Australia. The map below shows all of the continents. There are also smaller areas of land on Earth that are completely surrounded by water. These are called *islands*.

1. Which continent do you live on? Which continents are bigger than it is? Which ones are smaller?
2. Is North America or South America closer to Africa?
3. Which continent is the farthest south?
4. Which continents have the warmest weather? Which continents have the coolest weather? How do you know?
5. Australia is an interesting continent. Look at the map below. What do you notice about Australia?

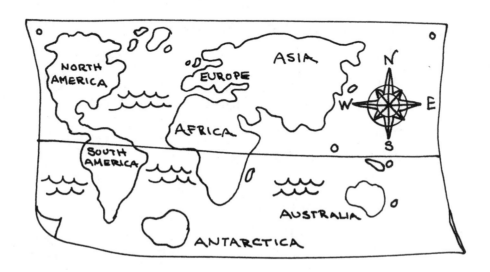

What is a synonym?

A synonym (SIH-nuh-nim) is a word that means the same, or almost the same thing, as another word. The following words are common synonyms: *large* and *big, fast* and *quick, happy* and *glad*. Each of these pairs of synonyms is made up of two words that have the same, or almost the same, meanings.

1. Look at the pictures on this page. What are two words, or synonyms, that tell what each picture means?

2. How many pairs of synonyms can you think of? Make a list of your synonym pairs on a separate piece of paper.

3. Can you draw a picture for each of your synonym pairs? Ask a friend to guess what they are.

4. Can you make up a funny story about synonyms? Perhaps it is about people living in a place called Synonym Town who each have two names, such as the Loud and Noisy Family or the Good-bye and Farewell Family. Try to use your own ideas as well.

5. Do you know what words that mean the opposite of each other are called?

What is a graph?

A graph is a picture or a diagram that shows certain information. By using pictures, numbers, and symbols, a graph makes it easy to sort out, or *organize*, information that has been collected. The different bits of information can then be compared. A graph could show the favorite foods, toys, or colors of the children in a group. There are lots of different ways to make a graph. The graph below is called a bar graph. A pie graph, or pie chart, is a circular graph that shows information by using lines to divide the "pie."

1. What kinds of graphs have you seen? What information was recorded in those graphs?
2. Look at the picture below. What kind of information is the girl organizing in this graph?
3. How many of the children in the graph have a cat as a pet?
4. Why is a graph a good way to organize information?
5. What kinds of information would be fun to collect and put in a graph? How would you get your information? How would you organize it in a graph?

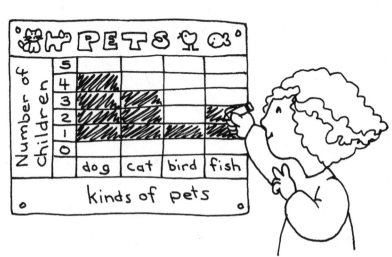

What is a collage?

A collage is a group of different drawings or pictures that are cut out from magazines and newspapers and pasted on one sheet of paper. The pictures can overlap one another, or they can be right next to each other. Usually, all the pictures in a collage have a common subject, or *theme*. You can make a collage of monster pictures, different kinds of flowers, or your favorite foods or toys.

1. Have you ever made a collage? What kinds of pictures did you use for it?
2. What types of things interest you? On a separate piece of paper, make a list of at least five subjects or things that you enjoy. Which subject would be the best to show in a collage? Why?

3. How would you make a word and picture collage of zoo animals? What types of words and pictures would you include?

4. Sometimes a collage is made with different materials, such as pieces of yarn or cloth. What other kinds of materials could you use to make a collage? Where would you look for materials to use in making a collage?

5. What other kinds of art projects do you enjoy doing?

GRADE BOOSTER!

Ask an adult to help you find magazines or newspapers that you can use to cut out pictures and words. Choose an idea for your collage and look through the magazines to find pictures and words that relate to your subject. Cut out the things you want and save them in an envelope. When you have collected enough pictures and words, start arranging them on a large piece of paper. Trim the pictures and words and experiment with how to place them on the paper. When you have a design that you like, carefully glue your cutouts to the paper to create your very own collage.

What do the stars on the American flag stand for?

The 50 stars on the American flag stand for, or *represent*, each one of the 50 states in the United States. The first American flag had 13 stars and 13 red-and-white stripes. These stood for the first 13 colonies, which later became states. As new states joined the United States, a new star was added for each one. The flag still has 13 stripes in honor of the first colonies.

1. Where do you usually see the American flag?

2. Look at the American flag shown below. How many rows of stars does the flag have? Are there the same number of stars in each row?

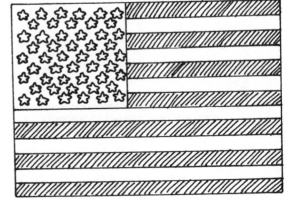

3. If more states join the United States, more stars will be added to the flag. How would you arrange 51 or 52 stars on the flag? On a separate piece of paper, draw an American flag with one or two more stars.

4. The flag of the Netherlands, a country in Europe, has three stripes. How many more stripes does the United States flag have? **Hint:** On a separate piece of paper, write out this subtraction problem: **13**
                                                       - 3

5. Why do you think there are stars on the American flag instead of another symbol?

What is an antonym?

An antonym (AN-tuh-nim) is a word that has the opposite meaning of another word. For example, *happy* is the antonym, or opposite, of *sad,* and *short* is the antonym of *tall.* Antonyms are the opposite of *synonyms,* which are words that mean the same thing.

1. Look at the pictures of the children playing. What are the antonyms that describe, or tell, where each child is on the see-saw and by the playhouse?

2. On a separate piece of paper, can you draw pictures that show the difference between the following antonyms?

open and **closed**   **full** and **empty**   **smooth** and **rough**

3. What are some other pairs of antonyms? Make a list of more antonym pairs on a separate piece of paper.
4. Can you draw pictures of your antonym pairs? Ask a friend to guess your antonyms.
5. Make up a sentence using each of your antonyms. Can you put those sentences together to tell a story?

What is a habitat?

A habitat is a place where certain people, animals, or plants usually live. Your habitat is the home where you live with your family. Some animals, such as bears and deer, make their homes and raise their families in the forest. The forest is their habitat. Wildflowers and big, tall redwood trees share this habitat. Some animals live in more than one habitat. For example, African elephants move back and forth from grassy areas called *grasslands* to the forest, because they eat both grass and tree parts. Different habitats can be found everywhere, even in the air or underground. National parks are protected habitats where many animals and plants are kept safe from people.

1. What is a whale's habitat? What other plants or animals share this habitat?
2. What is a wolf's habitat? What is an alligator's habitat? How are these habitats different from each other?
3. What animals live in very cold habitats, such as the Arctic? What do these animals look like?

4. What is your favorite animal? How is your habitat like that animal's habitat? How is it different?

5. Why do you think people provide protected habitats for plants and animals?

TOGETHER TIME: If possible, ask an adult to take you to the zoo. What kinds of animals can you see at the zoo? How do the people who work at the zoo make the animals' homes like their natural habitats? What differences do you see as you visit each animal's home at the zoo? If you do not live near a zoo, borrow some books on different animals from the library, or rent videos about animals. Be sure to make comparisons between the various animals and their homes.

What happens to water after it rains?

Most rain falls directly into the oceans, but some rain falls on land. Some of this rainwater runs off the land and into rivers and streams, which flow into the oceans. Other rainwater soaks into the ground and is used by plants and trees, which need water to live. A lot of rainwater simply *evaporates,* which means that it is pulled back into the sky as invisible vapor to form new clouds.

1. What things do you like to do on a rainy day when you can't play outside?
2. Rain is just one way that water falls from the sky. What other ways can you think of?
3. Like plants, people need water to live. What are some different ways you use water during the day?
4. What is a flood? If you don't know, how can you find out?
5. Put a small bowl of water in a sunny spot in the morning. Check the bowl at the end of the day. What happens to the water?

What does an astronaut do?

An astronaut is a person who pilots a spacecraft or works in space. Astronauts train for many years to travel into space. There are two kinds of astronauts that are selected for space flights. *Pilot* astronauts command and pilot the vehicles. The *mission specialist* astronauts take care of the equipment, do experiments, and perform space walks. Most American astronauts work for NASA, the government agency in charge of the United States space flights.

1. To become an astronaut, a person must love adventure. What does it mean to "love adventure"?

2. What do you think you might see at the space center in Houston, Texas, where most astronauts work?

3. A person must study very hard to become an astronaut. What subjects do you think an astronaut most needs to learn?

4. A space station is used as a base for astronauts who are staying in space for a long time. What do you think it would be like to live in a space station?

5. Can you imagine what a space station might look like? Draw one on a separate piece of paper.

What is geography?

The word *geography* means "a description of the Earth." People who study and learn about the surface of the Earth are called *geographers*. Geographers learn about all the different places on Earth, such as deserts, mountains, rivers, oceans, and continents. They describe where these things are located, what they look like, and how big they are. Geographers study people and how they live in an area, or environment. They also tell us about the plants and animals that can be found in these places.

1. Why would maps be important to a geographer?
2. A landmark is an object or a place that does not move from its position, such as a large oak tree or a school. What are some of the landmarks in your neighborhood that help you know when you are close to home?
3. Look carefully at a globe and point to where you live. What features does the globe show around that area? Do you live near an ocean? Are there any mountains nearby?

4. If you were a geographer, what part of the Earth would you most want to study?

5. Why do you think studying geography is important to people?

TOGETHER TIME: Play a fun geography game with an adult friend or a family member. Start with the first letter of the alphabet and name a continent, an ocean, a country, a state, a city, a town, a national park, a mountain range, a river, or a lake that starts with that letter. You may use a map or a globe to help you. Each player takes one turn at a time. Use a new letter each time one of you gives an answer. Ask the adult to keep track of each person's list of words on a separate piece of paper. If both of you are stumped, just move on to the next letter. The winner is the person with the most correct answers. Here are a few letters and names to start you off:

A Atlantic Ocean
B Boston
C California
D Denmark
E Europe

How do we know what money is worth?

Every country has its own kind of money, or *currency*. In the United States, the currency includes coins and paper bills. Each kind of money has a special design. Each piece also has the amount it is worth written on it. A penny is worth 1¢, a nickel is worth 5¢, a dime is worth 10¢, a quarter is worth 25¢, a half dollar is worth 50¢, and a dollar is worth 100¢, or $1. Paper money comes in bills for $1, $2, $5, $10, $20, $50, and $100. These pieces of currency are recognized and used everywhere in the United States.

1. Every coin shows the year that it was made. Can you find a coin that was made in the year that you were born?

2. Why do you think American coins come in different sizes?

3. Have you seen coins from other countries? What did they look like? What country were they from?

4. According to legend, pirates sometimes buried treasure chests full of coins and jewels. Why do you think they did this?

5. How much are a quarter, a nickel, a dime, and a penny worth altogether? **Hint:** On a separate piece of paper, write down how much each coin is worth, then add the numbers together.

Math

What is pollution?

Pollution is all of the ways that the Earth's environment, which includes air, water, and soil, has been hurt. For example, smoke from factories, exhaust from cars, and chemicals from fertilizers make the air, water, and soil dirty. This is harmful to plants and animals, as well as people, who need to live in a clean environment. People don't pollute on purpose, but pollution has happened over the years because of the way we live. Today, people are trying to find ways not to pollute the environment.

1. Have you ever seen pollution? Where did you see it? What does pollution look like?
2. What happens when oil from boats gets into an ocean or a lake?
3. If you and your friends are at a playground or a park, what can you do to help keep the area clean?
4. What is noise pollution?
5. Why do people *recycle,* or reuse, certain materials?

What is a calendar?

A calendar helps people keep track of time. It is a record of the days, weeks, and months of the year. A calendar usually shows the seven days of the week in order: Sunday, Monday, Tuesday, Wednesday, Thursday, Friday, and Saturday. It also shows each of the months. There are 12 months in a year. In order, the months are: January, February, March, April, May, June, July, August, September, October, November, and December. Each month has a certain number of days. For example, June has 30 days and December has 31 days. Because the months follow each other, it is possible for a new month to start in the middle of the week. Without a calendar, it would be very hard for us to keep track of the days.

1. On which days of the week do you go to school? On a separate piece of paper, make a list of the days on which you usually go to school.

2. How would a calendar help you remember someone's birthday?

3. Look at the calendar on this page. On which day of the week is September 11?

4. Check the calendar again. On which day of the week will the next month begin? What is the month after September?

SEPTEMBER

S	M	T	W	T	F	S
			1	2	3	4	5
6	7	8	9	10	11	12
13	14	15	16	17	18	19
20	21	22	23	24	25	26
27	28	29	30			

Math

5. Can you think of a reason why farmers need calendars?

TOGETHER TIME: Ask an adult to help you make your own calendar for this month. Find a calendar for this month that you can use as a model when you make your own. Get a large piece of paper and a pencil. At the top of the paper, write the name of the month. Below it, draw an outline of the calendar. Write the name of each day near the top of the outline. Be sure to start numbering the days in the correct square. Now you can fill in important information. Include any holidays or birthdays, and even when you have soccer practice or other activities. You can decorate your calendar as you wish.

How big is the ocean?

The ocean is too big to measure, but we know that this large body of water covers most of the Earth. Even though this water runs together, we think of it as four oceans and many smaller seas. The four oceans are the Pacific, the Atlantic, the Indian, and the Arctic. Near the seashore, where the land and water meet, the water is usually not very deep at all. Farther into the ocean, the water becomes much deeper. In some places, the water is so deep that sunlight cannot reach the bottom of the ocean!

1. Have you ever been to the ocean? Which one did you visit?
2. What kinds of animals live in the ocean?
3. Have you ever tasted ocean water? What did it taste like?
4. What do you think the bottom of the ocean is like?
5. Fill a dish with water. Lean down close to the dish. Take a deep breath and blow it out slowly. What happens? How is this like the waves on the ocean?

What is a homonym?

A homonym (HAH-muh-nim) is a word that sounds the same as another word but has a different spelling and meaning, or *definition*. Words like *hear* and *here* are homonyms because they have the same sound, but they are spelled differently and have different definitions.

1. On a separate piece of paper, can you draw a picture of each word in the homonym pairs below?

    hair and **hare**   **son** and **Sun**   **sail** and **sale**

2. Do you know what each of the homonyms above means? Ask an adult to help you write each definition on a separate piece of paper.

3. Can you make up a short story using all of the homonym pairs?

4. Can you think of more homonym pairs? On a separate piece of paper, draw pictures of three pairs of homonyms. Ask a friend to guess what the homonyms are.

5. Can you write a sentence using each pair of homonyms shown below?

chilly   chili   steak   stake

What are tropical rain forests?

Tropical rain forests are thick forests found all over the world, especially near the *equator,* the imaginary line around the middle of the Earth. Even though the Sun shines almost every day in a rain forest, thunder showers happen on more than 200 days a year. In a rain forest, the air is warm or hot, and damp. Tropical rain forests are filled with trees, bushes, vines, and ferns that stay green all year because there is so much rain. There are also many different kinds of animals that live in tropical rain forests.

1. It is usually dark near the floor of the rain forest. Why do you think that is?
2. In most areas, there is very little plant life on the tropical rain forest floor, but in some places jungles occur. What is a jungle? If you don't know, how can you find out?

3. Many trees are being cut down in rain forests all over the world. Why do you think people would cut down these trees?

4. When the trees in tropical rain forests are cut down, what do you think happens to the animals that live there?

5. Which continents have tropical rain forests? Which continents do not? **Hint:** Use the map below to help you.

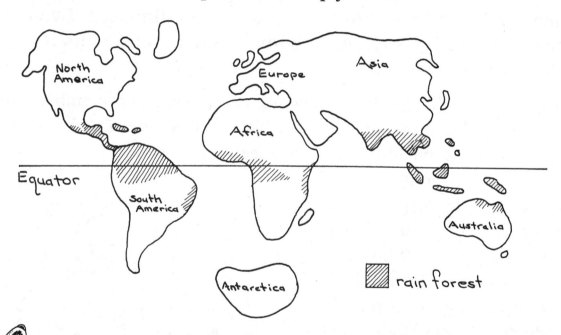

GRADE BOOSTER!

What kinds of plants and animals live in rain forests? To find out, you can use an encyclopedia or another book in the library. On a separate piece of paper, make a list of at least five plants and five animals that live in the tropical rain forests of the world. For extra fun, you can draw a picture of each plant or animal.

Why do people need to sleep?

People need to sleep in order to stay healthy. While you sleep, your body recovers from all of the hard work it has done during the day, and it gets new energy for the next day. If you do not get enough sleep, your body will be too tired to work properly. You may not be able to concentrate or think clearly. You are also more likely to get sick, because as you sleep, your body is able to fight off many illnesses. Even when you rest quietly, your body is not as relaxed as it is when you are asleep.

1. People often dream when they are asleep. Do you remember any of the dreams that you have had? Can you describe one?
2. Why might it be difficult to fall asleep if you feel excited or scared?
3. Most people sleep for a long time at night and are awake during the day. Why do you think that is? Do you know anyone who sleeps more during the day than at night?

4. Why do you think babies sleep so much?
5. What other things besides sleep should people do to stay healthy?

Does it ever rain in the desert?

It does rain in the desert, but not very much. A desert is a place where only certain plants and animals can live because there is so little water. We often think of deserts as hot, dry places where sand stretches for miles. Some deserts do fit this description, but there are actually many different kinds of deserts around the world. These deserts can have rocks, some grass, and mountains. Others can be scattered with trees, shrubs, cactuses, and other plants.

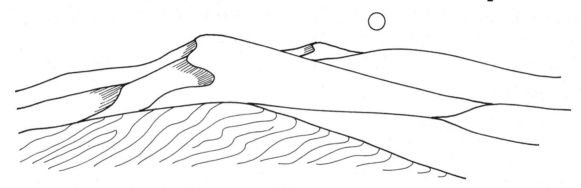

1. What animals live in a desert? How can they live in a place with little or no water?
2. Do you think many people live in the desert?
3. In some places, desert winds blow the sand into hills called *sand dunes*. Look at the picture above. What do the sand dunes look like to you?
4. What places can you think of that get a lot of rain? What is it like there?
5. On a separate piece of paper, make a picture of a desert using different materials. What can you use to show the sand, the Sun, and any animals or plants?

What did children do for fun long ago?

Children in the past played games very much like the games children play today. In 1200 B.C., Egyptian children played catch with each other and tug-of-war. Children living in Rome in 120 A.D. often played marbles. During the cold Norway winters of 950 A.D., Viking children skated on frozen rivers and threw snowballs at each other. During the 1200–1400s, some European children learned archery. Children in India during the 1600s played a board game that is like today's Parcheesi game. In the mid-1800s, English children played checkers and dominoes. Native American children during the 1700s and 1800s played with dolls made from buffalo skins.

1. Look at the pictures on these pages. What games are children of long ago playing that children of today still play?
2. What things do you do for fun that children long ago used to do?

3. How do you think we know what children living in other times learned and what they liked to do for fun?

4. How could you find out more about the different games children in the past played?

5. What do you think children in the future will do for fun? On a separate piece of paper, draw a picture of some toys of the future.

TOGETHER TIME: Ask an adult to help you draw a timeline filled with pictures of the things children have done for fun from ancient times through today. Be sure that you write the correct dates along your timeline. **Hint:** Use the information on these pages to help you. Where will you put yourself on the timeline? What will you draw to show the things you play with and the games you are learning? Ask your adult friend what games and fun activities he or she enjoyed playing as a child. Where will you put this adult on the timeline? How will you draw the games and activities he or she liked to play?

What is the Statue of Liberty?

The Statue of Liberty is a very large sculpture that stands on Liberty Island at the entrance to New York harbor. It was a gift from the people of France to the people of the United States. The Statue of Liberty reminds people of the belief that Americans have in independence and freedom. It is a symbol of hope for many people who move to the United States. The statue is over 151 feet tall. It is so big that you can walk around inside it. The crown on the statue's head contains 25 windows that people can look out of. Each year, about two million people visit the Statue of Liberty.

1. How tall are you? If you don't know, ask an adult to measure your height.

2. If you climbed to the top of the Statue of Liberty and looked down, how would the ground look?

3. What does the word **liberty** mean? If you don't know, how can you find out?

4. Why do you think the people of France gave the Statue of Liberty to the people of the United States?

5. Why do you think that a statue was a good gift for one country to give to another country?

ANSWERS

Page 5

1. There are seven days in each week.
2. Sample answers: In floor or wall tiles, in wallpaper, in a patterned carpet, and in the material of patterned curtains, bedding, and upholstery.
3–4. Answers will vary.
5. Sample answer: You could show your friend how to hop two times on one foot, then, standing still, say the word **Hop!** two times. Repeat this action and word pattern several times, so your friend can learn it.

Pages 6–7

1. It would be better to estimate the number of stars you see in the sky because there will probably be too many to count.
2. No, you cannot see stars during the day. They are still there, but sunlight makes the sky too bright to see them.
3. A star map is a map that shows where certain stars or constellations (groups of stars) are.
4. Sample answer: Having a telescope in space would give astronomers a better view of stars and other galaxies than they have from Earth.
5. Answers will vary.
TT: Without a telescope, you can see many stars in the sky, but they look very small. Through a telescope, you can see many more stars, and they appear to be much larger and closer.

Page 8

1. Answers will vary.
2. No, animals do not talk the way people do, but many animals are able to communicate by using sounds, and especially by moving their bodies in certain ways. This is called *body language*.
3. Sample answer: By pointing to things or drawing pictures to show what you mean.
4. Sign language is a system of hand gestures that are used to communicate with others, especially by deaf people.
5. Most people who live in France speak French. You can look it up in an encyclopedia.

Page 9

1. Answers will vary.
2. Sample answers: The rain, wind, or a running brook.
3. Sample answers: In movies, on the radio, at parties, during parades, at the circus, or at religious services.
4. Sample answer: The rhythm of the music makes them feel happy.
5. Sample answers: Stage plays or operas.

Pages 10–11

1. Answers will vary.
2. From the price tag or a sign.
3. Sample answers: It is a container in a pig shape inside which you can keep money. People save money so that they can buy the things they really want or need.
4. Sample answer: They traded whatever they had. People made different things depending on where they lived and what materials they had.
5. Answers will vary.

Page 12

1. Presidents' Day is on the third Monday in February.
2. Washington, D.C. You can look on a map or in an encyclopedia.
3. **Parent:** Check answer to be sure that it is correct.
4. Sample answer: As a father might care for his family, Washington helped create the strong government that runs the United States.
5. Answers will vary.

Page 13

1. No. If the cloud meets warm air, the drops of water will evaporate again and the cloud will disappear.
2. Sample answer: They are dark.
3. Fog is a cloud that is close to the ground.
4. Dew is usually seen on the leaves of plants or on grass. It is moisture that can form overnight when plants and temperatures may cool down.
5. Sample answers: Weather is the way we describe the atmosphere— whether it's cloudy or clear, hot or cold, wet or dry, calm or stormy outside. A dark cloud might tell us that it's stormy out or that a storm is coming. Moving clouds might tell us that it's windy.

Pages 14–15

1. The one on the left is a dial clock. The one on the right is a digital clock. According to the clocks, it is 8:00.
2. **Parent:** Check answer to be sure that it is correct.
3. Sample answer: So they can easily and conveniently check the time.
4. Sample answers: To see when it's time for school, when a TV show will be on, when it's time for dinner, when it's time to meet someone, or when it's time for bed.
5. Sample answer: Your heartbeat is not as consistent as the ticking of a clock. For example, your heart may beat faster when you exercise than when you are sitting still.

Page 16

1. Sample answer: So that people can react quickly, because symbols are easy to recognize.
2. Sample answers: Sheet music, money, weather maps, or in houses of worship, such as temples and churches.
3–4. Answers will vary.
5. Some of these pieces of stone and pottery still exist today.

Page 17

1. **Equator** comes from a Latin word meaning "to equalize." It divides the Earth into equal parts.
2. The equator runs through South America, Africa, and islands that are part of Asia.
3. The United States is north of the equator. You can use a globe, a world map, or an atlas to check your answer.
4. Because the equator circles the widest part of the Earth, it is close to the Sun most of the time.
5. ½

Pages 18–19

1. Answers will vary.
2. Sample answers: Independence Day or New Year's Eve. The noise, colors, and patterns of fireworks make them exciting to watch.
3. Sample answer: To show thanks for everything they have, including the food they eat and good friends.
4–5. Answers will vary.

Page 20

1. **Pancake, firefly,** and **doghouse**.
2. **Butter** and **fly; side** and **walk; grand** and **father**.
3–4. Answers will vary.
5. Sample answers: Dollhouse, houseboat, housework, greenhouse, lighthouse, schoolhouse, housekeeper.

Page 21

1. Sample answer: A flag would stand as a symbol of how the 13 colonies worked together and fought for independence from England during the Revolutionary War.
2. A legend is a story from the past, especially one that is thought to be historical but cannot be proven. A legend is also a key to the symbols used on a map or a chart.
3. Sample answer: No information about who designed and made the flag was written down at the time.
4. Sample answer: The Olympic flag, which stands for the Olympic Games held every two years.
5. Answers will vary.

Pages 22–23

1. Sample answers: It smells sweet, tastes tangy, feels sticky, looks orange, and sounds squishy.
2. Sight. A blind person touches raised letter characters called Braille.
3. Sight, hearing, and touch. Sample answer: No. It is possible for someone who is blind to learn how to play the piano.
4. Answers will vary.
5. Sample answers: You can hear people yelling, taste spoiled milk, smell smoke, feel the heat from a stove, and see an emergency exit.

Page 24

1. Answers will vary.
2. Sample answer: When you are going on vacation.
3. Sample answers: As a circle with the letters **N, S, E,** and **W** marked around the circle, or as intersecting arrows.
4. Sample answers: A globe is round to show the shape of the Earth. A map is flat. A globe always shows the entire world, but a map may show more detail for a specific area. You should use a map to see how to get to the park because a globe does not show that much detailed information.
5. Answers will vary.

Page 25

1. Answers will vary.
2. Sample answers: Many settlers believed that owning land was a source of wealth and independence. Many Native Americans believed that land could not be owned exclusively, but could be used instead as needed. You can look it up in an encyclopedia.
3. Sample answers: The word **bravery** means "showing courage." Pocahontas felt strongly about helping John Smith and creating peace between the settlers and the Native Americans.
4. Sample answers: Corn, beads, blankets, hides and furs, European tools.
5. You can look it up in an encyclopedia or another book at the library.

Page 26

1. **Can** and **not; can't**.
2–3. Answers will vary.
4. ***Parent:*** Child should write **don't; do** and **not**; circle the second **o**; and add an apostrophe between **n** and **t**. Also, **hasn't; has** and **not**; circle the **o**; and add an apostrophe between the **n** and **t**. Also, **she'll; she** and **will**; circle **wi**; and add an apostrophe between the **e** and the first **l**.
5. Sample answer: Contractions are more informal and easier to say.

Page 27

1. A playhouse that is built in a tree.
2. No, a tree probably does not feel any pain because it does not have a brain or nerves.
3. Sample answer: Trees are generally taller and live longer than other plants.
4. Sample answers: Free and knee.
5. Sample answer: Trees are an important part of the Earth, but many trees are cut down so that we can use the wood. People want to make sure these trees are replaced.

Pages 28–29

1. Answers will vary.
2. **Fair** and **ware; Simon** and **pieman; penny** and **any**.
3. Answers will vary.
4. **Ware** is usually an item for sale. It is the pie in this rhyme.
5. Sample answer: It is more fun to believe that Mother Goose was real.
GB: Sample answers: Bat, hat, mat, pat, rat, sat. Rest of answer will vary.

Page 30

1. Answers will vary.
2. No, they should make different sounds because they are different sizes. The largest bottle should make the lowest sound.
3. Answers will vary.
4. You play a wind instrument by blowing air into it. You play a stringed instrument by plucking the strings or by moving a bow across the strings.
5. Sample answer: When different instruments are played together, the sounds complement each other, or sound nice all together.

Page 31

1. Answers will vary.
2. Sample answer: They could choose any place they wanted to set up their new home, the area was not as crowded, and there was more farmland available.
3. It was much safer than traveling alone, the people could share food and other supplies, and they could help each other.
4. Answers will vary.
5. Sample answer: Because they are curious and interested in exploring someplace new.

Pages 32–33

1. Answers will vary.
2. Sample answers: Work in a zoo or a botanical garden, or in a school or a research laboratory.
3. It is a microscope. Sample answer: A plant cell or other very small objects.
4. Sample answer: National parks have lots of plants and animals living in their natural habitats.
5. Sample answers: Chemistry and astronomy. By looking in an encyclopedia under **science**.

Page 34

1. Sample answers: The tortoise was slow, steady, and didn't give up. The hare was fast and overly confident.
2. Sample answer: He stopped too long. He thought that because he could run fast, he could rest and still win.
3. Sample answer: Steady, hard work and staying focused on a task are what you need to be successful.
4–5. Answers will vary.

Page 35

1. Sample answers: If you live in North America, Asia and Africa are bigger. South America, Antarctica, Europe, and Australia are smaller.

2. South America.
3. Antarctica.
4. Sample answers: South America and Africa might be very warm, while Antarctica might be cold. Areas near the equator are usually the warmest.
5. Sample answer: Australia is also an island. Australia is considered a continent because it is a large land mass.

Page 36

1. **Sick** and **ill**; **yelling** and **shouting**.
2–4. Answers will vary.
5. Antonyms.

Page 37

1. Answers will vary.
2. Information about the number and kinds of pets children have.
3. Three.
4. Sample answer: A graph puts different bits of information together in one place so that it is easy to study and compare the information.
5. Sample answer: The number of children in class who walk to school, ride the school bus, or get a ride from an adult. Rest of answer will vary.

Pages 38–39

1. Answers will vary.
2. *Parent:* Answers will vary, but child should choose the one that would be easiest to show with magazine cutouts.
3. Sample answers: By cutting out pictures of zoo animals, as well as words that name or describe zoo animals, then arranging and gluing the pictures and words on a sheet of paper. Rest of answer will vary.
4. Answers will vary.
5. Sample answers: Painting or drawing.

Page 40

1. Sample answers: At a school, a post office, or a baseball field.
2. The American flag has nine rows of stars. Not all the rows have the same number of stars. Five rows have six stars, and four rows have five stars.
3. Answers will vary.
4. 10.
5. Stars were used because the original 13 colonies were considered to be the bright, shining stars of a new country being created in a new land.

Page 41

1. **Up** and **down**; **in** and **out**.
2–5. Answers will vary.

Pages 42–43

1. A whale's habitat is the open ocean. Rest of answer will vary.
2. Sample answer: A wolf's habitat is in the forests and an alligator's habitat is in the wetlands. Rest of answer will vary.
3. Sample answers: Polar bears, penguins, seals, and walruses. Rest of answer will vary.
4. Sample answers: Your habitat is like the habitat of squirrels because both you and squirrels live in homes that give protection from danger and bad weather. Your habitat is different from the habitat of squirrels because you live in a building, while squirrels live in nests in trees.
5. Sample answer: People have destroyed some habitats by hunting animals and cutting down trees. Other people are trying to help these animals and plants survive.

Page 44

1. Answers will vary.
2. Sample answers: Hail, sleet, and snow.
3. Sample answers: For drinking, cooking, bathing, washing clothes, and swimming in.
4. Floods occur when the ground is too wet to absorb any more water, or when the water level of rivers or lakes rises above their banks or shores. You can look it up in a dictionary.
5. Some of the water evaporates.

Page 45

1. Sample answer: A person enjoys exploring new and different, sometimes dangerous, things.
2. Answers will vary.
3. Sample answers: Math, physics, and astronomy.
4–5. Answers will vary.

Pages 46–47

1. Sample answer: Geographers use maps to show the information they have gathered or to get information about areas they are interested in.
2. Sample answers: Stores, gas stations, parks, signs, and many more places and objects.
3–4. Answers will vary.
5. Sample answer: People want to learn more about the world they live in and how it changes.

Page 48

1. Answers will vary.
2. Sample answer: The different sizes make the coins easy to identify.

3. Answers will vary.
4. Sample answers: The chests were too big and heavy to take on board the ships when they sailed off to other places. They also didn't want other pirates to steal their "loot."
5. 41¢

Page 49

1. Sample answers: Pollution may be black smoke, smog in the sky, a garbage dump, or it can be invisible.
2. Sample answer: The oil makes the water dirty, and this makes it hard for plants and animals to live in that water.
3. Sample answer: Pick up any litter you see and toss it into a trash can.
4. Sample answer: Too much noise from traffic and machinery, which can reduce the quality of life for people.
5. Sample answer: Recycling helps the environment by reducing the amount of solid waste that has to be dumped or burned.

Pages 50–51

1. Monday, Tuesday, Wednesday, Thursday, and Friday.
2. Sample answer: You could write the birthday on the calendar and check the calendar regularly.
3. Friday.
4. Thursday. October.
5. Sample answer: To plan for their crops and keep track of the different growing seasons.

Page 52

1. Answers will vary.
2. Sample answers: Dolphins, fish, and eels.
3. Ocean water, or seawater, tastes very salty.
4. Sample answer: It is like land, with canyons and mountains.
5. Sample answer: The air creates little ripples on the water. The ocean waves are also caused by air moving over the water.

Page 53

1. Answers will vary.
2. Sample answers: Hair is the material that grows on the outside of your head and your body; a hare is an animal similar to a rabbit. A son is a male child of a man and a woman; the Sun is the star around which the Earth and other planets orbit in space. A sail is a piece of material that catches the wind and makes a sailboat move; a sale is where different things are sold.

3–5. Answers will vary.

Pages 54–55

1. Sample answer: The canopy layer of tree leaves is so thick that it blocks out all the light.
2. Sample answer: A jungle is a dense growth of plant life in a tropical rain forest in areas where a lot of sunlight reaches the ground. By looking in an encyclopedia or in a book at the library.
3. Sample answer: To use the wood to make other things.
4. Sample answer: The animals lose their homes, as well as shelter from other animals.
5. North America, South America, Africa, Asia, and Australia have rain forests. Europe and Antarctica do not.

GB: Sample answers: Rosewood trees, mahogany trees, kapoks, figs, and palms; bats, lizards, sloths, tapirs, and toucans.

Page 56

1. Answers will vary.
2. Sample answer: If you are excited or scared, it is difficult for your body to relax enough to fall asleep.
3. Sample answer: People are used to sleeping at night because it is easier to work during daylight hours. Rest of answer will vary.
4. Sample answer: Babies sleep a lot because their bodies need the energy to grow at a fast pace.
5. Sample answers: Eat a healthy diet and exercise.

Page 57

1. Sample answers: Camels, lizards, horned toads, desert turtles, rattlesnakes, jackrabbits, scorpions, snakes, and roadrunners. Many of these animals keep out of the hot sun during the day by sleeping under rocks or burrowing under the ground. All of them can live without much water.
2. No, not very many people live in the desert because people need water to live.
3. Sample answer: Ocean waves.
4. Sample answer: A tropical rain forest, where there are lots of trees and the air is very warm and damp.
5. Sample answers: Use sandpaper for sand, yellow cellophane for the Sun, brown felt for a camel, and green felt for a cactus.

Pages 58–59

1. They are playing catch and a board game called checkers.
2. Answers will vary.
3. Sample answer: Archaeologists have discovered actual objects and other clues from the past that tell us this information.
4. Sample answers: By looking in books at a library, or by going to a museum that shows these games on exhibit.
5. Answers will vary.

Page 60

1. Answers will vary.
2. Sample answer: The ground would be very far away and the people walking on it would look tiny.
3. **Liberty** means "the quality or state of being free." You can look it up in a dictionary.
4. Sample answer: It was an expression of friendship because both countries share a belief in liberty.
5. Sample answer: A statue is relatively permanent, so people would be able to enjoy it for many, many years.